# The Well Armed Woman's Concise Guide To Concealed Carry

Carrie Lightfoot

# DEDICATION

This book is dedicated to Ruth.
To meet Ruth,
Visit
http://www.thewellarmedwoman.com/blog/never-forget-ruth

# CONTENTS

# WELCOME

You are awesome and I am so thrilled to see you here. It shows
your commitment to acquiring the information, training and
gear to be a responsible Well Armed Woman.

Your journey to becoming your own self-protector begins and
ends with you, not with the gun in your hands or the holster on
your hip. It is important to lay down a firm and solid foundation of
knowledge and understanding of all that is involved with carrying a
concealed firearm.  From this solid base, you can make informed
decisions on everything from safety choices holster choice.

Here you will find concise, no-nonsense information that I hope
assists you as you move forward as a woman gun owner. I, along
with all the resources at **The Well Armed Woman** are here to
help you every step of the way.

# 1 CONCEALED CARRY BASICS

Conceal and Carry, Concealed Carry, or CCW, is defined as the carrying of a handgun or other weapon in public in a concealed manner, either on one's person or in proximity. The Supreme Court, in District of Columbia v. Heller (2008), ruled that the Second Amendment protects "the individual right to possess and carry weapons in case of confrontation". Self-defense is a fundamental right, and currently, all 50 states have laws that allow citizens to carry certain concealed firearms in public. The laws of all states also recognize the right to use arms in self-defense, but because the laws vary and are subject to change, it is imperative that you know the laws in your state and how they apply to you, in and out of your home.

It is your responsibility to not only understand the concealed carry laws but also understand the seriousness of the responsibility you assume when you choose to carry concealed. As intelligent women we instinctively know that we need to protect ourselves, and that the world we live in, sadly, requires us to continually be aware of our surroundings, and to know that there are potentially some very bad people out there who may do us harm. We as women are traditionally nurturers and life givers, not life takers. This can be a difficult thing to reconcile but we must each make our own personal determination about what we would be willing to do to survive or protect a loved one in the event of a life threatening situation.

The decision to conceal and carry shouldn't be taken lightly. There needs to be careful consideration of all the available information --- awareness of the laws, understanding of safety issues, thorough training, along with some deep soul searching. We owe it to ourselves to understand the serious emotional, social and legal ramifications of carrying a gun, and, possibly, pulling the trigger. Take the time to research, understand, and make the right decision for you.

Carrying a concealed gun means taking on great responsibility, not only for your own safety, but for the safety of those around you. It is essential that you be fully trained in how to use it. If you are not prepared to wholeheartedly commit to this, than you are not ready for the responsibility of gun ownership. In a later chapter I'll discuss how and where you can get good training geared to your specific needs as a woman. Luckily there is a growing and enthusiastic community of female gun owners ready and waiting to help and support you.

For women, carrying a concealed firearm poses some significant and unique challenges. Besides the legal and moral issues that must be dealt with there are some logistical hurdles as well. As opposed to men, for instance, our curvy bodies and close-fitting clothing styles can make it difficult to locate a concealed holster. Having children in the home or on the hip will dictate many of the choices and decisions surrounding concealed carry issues.

A truly well-armed woman will be armed with the facts, a thorough understanding of the ethical and legal issues, impeccable training, and an acute awareness of how carrying a firearm fits into her particular lifestyle. We'll touch on each of these topics more in-depth in the following chapters.

# 2 HOW TO OBTAIN YOUR CONCEALED CARRY PERMIT

I receive many questions from women about how to obtain a permit to carry a concealed firearm. Whether it's for their own personal protection, their family's protection, or just for a little added peace of mind, an increasing number of women throughout the country are considering applying for a permit to carry a concealed gun. The permitting procedure is different for every state. Below is some useful information to help you get started in applying for your CCW permit.

First, you will need to check out the laws of the state in which you want to get the permit. The National Rifle Association's website (NRA-ILA.org) is an excellent resource for up to the minute information on gun laws, state by state. There are three types of jurisdictions when it comes to issuing a concealed carry permit:

- **Shall-Issue:** Most states are 'shall-issue' jurisdictions, in which permits to carry a concealed gun will be granted (shall be issued) if certain predetermined criteria are met. There is no requirement that you show good cause for the need for a CCW permit.

- **May-Issue:** 'May-issue' jurisdictions require a permit to carry a concealed gun, but permits are granted at the discretion of the issuing authority. In addition to meeting specified criteria, you may also be asked to demonstrate 'good cause' to carry a concealed gun – and self-defense alone does not meet this requirement in most jurisdictions. In some may-issue states, CCW permits are arbitrarily denied without any reason given for the denial. At this time, may-issue states include California, Connecticut, Delaware, Hawaii,* Maryland, Massachusetts, New Jersey, New York, and Rhode Island.

    * Check status – currently in U.S. 9th Circuit Court of Appeals

- **No-Issue:** A 'no-issue' jurisdiction does not grant CCW permits to private citizens. Although currently the only no-issue jurisdiction in the U.S. is the District of Columbia, several may-issue states, including Hawaii, Maryland, and New Jersey, are effectively no-issue states in practice because so many permits are arbitrarily denied.

Regardless of the type of jurisdiction (with the exception of Washington D.C.), there are basic some steps you'll need to take to apply for your permit:

1. Identify the permitting authority in your state or jurisdiction, and request CCW permit application materials.
2. Completely fill out all application paperwork. Make sure to double-check every document you submit, as failing to fill it out completely can cause delay or outright denial of your permit application.
3. Pay the required fees. The application fees are typically lower for residents of the jurisdiction, so make sure you are applying to the correct jurisdiction to minimize costs

associated with getting a CCW permit.

4. Take gun safety or firearms training courses. Some jurisdictions require that you pass a safety training class before you will be eligible for a CCW permit, but proper training should be received regardless of whether or not it is required in your jurisdiction. Make sure to complete all necessary courses prior to submitting your application.

Taking special care to identify and follow all the rules and regulations associated with applying for a concealed carry permit in your state will help ensure that your application is successful.

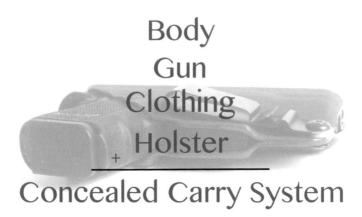

Body
Gun
Clothing
+ Holster
Concealed Carry System

# 3 BUILDING YOUR CONCEALED CARRY SYSTEM

Once you've researched the gun laws in your state and applied for your permit, you are ready to begin building your own personal concealed carry system…a system made up of your gun, your body, your clothing, and your holster(s). They must all work together seamlessly for a truly safe and effective concealed carry.

There are several key elements that are necessary for optimal comfort and safety. Choosing a gun is the first and most important decision you will make because your gun is the central piece of equipment that all other parts of your system must work around. It should be the right size for you, fitting both your hand and your body as a whole. When you find the right fit, training will be easier, carrying will be comfortable, and shooting will be safe.

Finding 'your' gun really isn't all that complicated, but it can be challenging for a new shooter who lacks experience and confidence. Every woman is unique, and there are certainly a lot of options out there when it comes to purchasing a gun. But by following a few simple guidelines, you will not only find the right gun for you, but you will do it with confidence. Here are some simple questions that will serve as a guide to help you find the right match:

**1. Do I want a revolver or semi-automatic pistol?**

Factors such as hand strength, finger strength, ammunition capacity and mechanical complexity must all be considered in order to answer this question. Physically the two types of guns are very different, and offer very different shooting 'styles'. Can you effectively pull the trigger of a double action revolver or 'rack' the slide of the semi-automatic pistol? Does one feel more natural in your hand than the other? You will have to try them out to answer that question.

Revolvers have a cylinder with multiple chambers, and each chamber holds a round of ammunition. Most models hold 5 or 6 rounds. Pulling the trigger rotates the cylinder and aligns the loaded chamber with the barrel and the gun then fires. A revolver is a very simple machine, therefore there is little that can go wrong with the firing process. This makes a revolver a good and reliable choice for self defense, although they are heavier and bulkier than semi-automatic pistols and tend to hold fewer rounds. And while all guns should be cleaned regularly, the simplicity of these mechanics makes the effectiveness of a revolver less dependent on meticulous cleaning. Another thing to note is that revolvers have a long and hard trigger pull which makes it very difficult to accidentally pull the trigger; this acts as a safety feature, but finger strength must be taken into account.

A semi-automatic pistol is a handgun where the magazine which holds the ammunition slides into the grip of the gun. A semi-automatic pistol uses the energy created from firing the gun to eject the spent cartridge and load a fresh one. Semi-automatic pistols typically hold a larger number of rounds, which can be a significant factor in self-protection. Semi-automatics also generally have an easier trigger pull, have the ability to shoot multiple rounds very quickly, and are slimmer and more compact in shape. Semi-automatic pistols, however, are not as mechanically simple as revolvers and require regular and thorough cleaning to insure proper function. Their semi-automatic action is dependent on the first round firing successfully so the next round is cycled into the chamber. That being said, the reliability of modern semi-automatic pistols is exceptionally high.

### 2. What caliber handgun should you get?

Which caliber is best for your self-defense? For self-defense, the best caliber for you is the one you can shoot and manage comfortably, and that can do the most damage to stop a threat. For many women it will be a question of what caliber they can handle safely and effectively. But remember, a handgun of ANY caliber is better than none

Smaller handgun calibers such as .22, .25, .30, and .32 are usually not recommended for self-defense because the bullet size is considered too small to inflict enough damage to stop an attacker. You would have to shoot multiple, and very accurate, shots to be effective, and even then it might not be enough to stop a larger attacker, or one who is under the influence of drugs or alcohol. Of course there are exceptions, but it's something to think about.

Ideally, for self-defense, a caliber of .380 in a semi automatic pistol or .38 Special in a revolver would be the lowest caliber to consider. But again, any gun of any caliber is better than none, so a new shooter may want to start off with a lower caliber gun and work her way up as her skill level improves. If you just can't manage the higher calibers, try a .22 and work your way up.

This is a simplified overview to assist the new shooter, and there is much to learn about ammunition, caliber and the ballistics of different types of ammunition. I encourage you to take some time to explore these subjects.

### 3. How does it fit in your hand?

Whichever type of gun you are considering, your hand should comfortably wrap the entirety of the grip, giving you a strong secure handle on it. You should be able to perform the mechanical operations of the gun confidently, including pulling the hammer back on a single action revolver or pressing the magazine release button and releasing the slide lock on a semi-automatic pistol. The meat or pad of your finger should lie solidly and comfortably on the trigger. If you have to stretch or change your grip on the handgun to accomplish this, then it's not the right gun for you.

### 4. How will YOUR body best carry a concealed gun?

This is a very important question to answer. Body shape, size, and how you dress are all important factors in selecting your gun. Let's be honest, a 32A bust size will not conceal a Glock 19 in a bra holster very well! Physical limitations must be considered as well, such as your ability to bend or reach. Being pregnant, or a larger size, brings a new set of issues. We'll discuss this in more detail in later chapters.

### 5. Most importantly – take it for a test drive if you can!

Many ranges and gun shops have rentals or demo guns so that you can get a feel for different options before you commit to buy. Try to locate one, even if it means driving a bit of a distance. If you have friends who own guns, perhaps they can take you shooting with them. Finding the opportunity to shoot different types of guns of different calibers is the ideal final step in selecting the right gun for you. As with any fine machine, each make and model will have significant differences, and getting the chance to experience them up close and personal makes for the most successful selection.

My hope is that you begin the task of finding this partner in self-protection with a sense of confidence. These guidelines should give you an idea of what you want, and how to identify the right gun for you. The final decision is one only you can make.

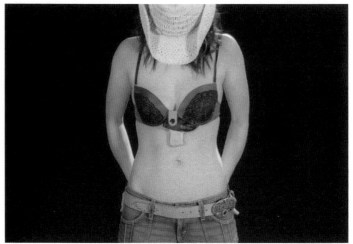

# 4 ABOUT CONCEALED CARRY HOLSTERS FOR WOMEN

"Carrying a gun isn't supposed to be comfortable, it is supposed to be a comfort"  Clint Smith

Clint's quote above is very revealing and it is important to understand that concealed carry for a women inevitably means making some physical adjustments and concessions. There may be times when it's an inconvenience or a little uncomfortable, but this just comes with the territory. You are choosing to carry a serious piece of equipment on your person, and feeling it on your body is a healthy reminder of the awesome responsibility to handle it with care and respect. With time, you will feel naked without your gun on you, and if you are ever required to use it to save your life, believe me it will be well worth the little bit of discomfort.

On the body carrying is the safest and best way for you to carry your gun. When it is held against your body you can easily access your gun, but others can't. The problem is that most holsters are made for men, and most men's holsters simply don't work with a woman's physique. They can be uncomfortable and downright unsafe.

Just because a holster is pink, it's no guarantee that it was designed for a women's body. And even though the industry is finally making some progress in addressing these issues, finding a holster designed for a woman is extremely difficult both online and in gun stores. **The Well Armed Woman** has taken on this challenge; we've sought out the best options and designed an exclusive line of holsters for women. Every female shooter deserves to have a full selection of holsters designed specifically with her body and her lifestyle in mind. It's not only a matter of comfort, it affects the functionality and the safety of your gun.

Whether you carry in your pocket, in a purse, or in your belt, your firearm *must be holstered* and the *trigger covered at all times*. Be careful of holsters that do not fully cover the trigger guard. A good holster is one that is designed specifically for your gun, either your specific model, or for its type and size. It should hold the gun securely --- not too tight that it is difficult to remove, and not too loose that it slides out on its own. A good holster is one that attaches to your body or clothing securely, and is comfortable. This is a very important piece of equipment in your self defense plan, it is not intended to be "sexy" or pretty. It has a very important job to do and so the focus has to be on performance, not appearance.

There are several challenges that present themselves when we try to address the issue of concealing a gun on a woman's body. Part of it is physiological...a woman's body is curvy and a gun is, well, not! The other part has to do with fashion. Women tend to wear more fitted styles and many of the fabrics we love are thin and sheer. Dresses pose an additional set of challenges, as does the absence of a belt. Yet, to provide the security we desire, our gun must be close, accessible, and hidden from view.

This is where it gets challenging for women, as so many holsters are designed for a man's body. Our hips are typically larger and sit at a different angle than a man's hips. An ill fitting holster on a woman will jut the butt of the gun out, making it difficult to conceal. Because our waists are shorter, a holster designed for a man will sit up higher on the waistband, leaving little or no room to draw the gun without our underarm or bust interfering. Wearing low rise jeans can help to minimize this lack of space by creating a bit more space for drawing.

Your choice of clothing is critical if you intend to carry concealed. Your clothing not only needs to fit you, it needs to fit your gun. Does it cover the gun completely? Are there any bulges? These are all important considerations. Men have it easy! Their wardrobe consists of pants and a shirt, only the style and fabrics change. Women on the other hand wear a variety of different clothing styles and fashion is very important to us. You may be thinking that you aren't willing to give up your sense of style to accommodate a concealed carry handgun, and you shouldn't have to.

Likely, some concessions and changes will be necessary but with a variety of holster options carried in some creative locations, many of these challenges can be addressed. Different types of holsters will work with different clothing styles, and are appropriate for varied activities. Think about how you dress most often and begin to plan your strategy.

Here are some specific clothing ideas that might be helpful:

- Wear low rise jeans and pants to increase the available space to draw from the waistband.
- Buy your pants and skirts with a little more room in the waistband to accommodate your new bulge.
- Wear patterned clothing to help hide bulge and minimize the printing of the outline of your gun in your clothing.
- Wear boot cut or looser legged pants to accommodate an ankle holster.
- Wear flowing, looser shirts for better bulge coverage, especially for bra, belly band or underarm carry.
- Wear a sleeveless light long vest. These are great for small of the back carry, and depending on the fabric, can be worn year round.
- Don't forget your boots--- they can fit a small firearm nicely. Clip an in-the-waist holster right down the inside of your boot.

Your gun, holsters, clothing and body, are all important components of your concealed carry system and, if matched appropriately, will work in unison to keep you comfortable, confident, and safe.

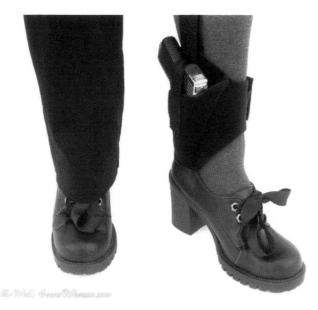

# 5 HOLSTER OPTIONS FOR WOMEN

Here are the most common options for effective conceal and carry, ordered by location on the body:

### On The Waistband Carry - OWB

Belt carry or on-the-waist carry, is the preferred and most common form of concealed carry for women because of the easy access it provides. The gun is close and the grip is in a great position to grasp and draw quickly. This type of concealment can be accomplished in two ways: outside the waistband or inside the waistband.

**Outside the waistband** holsters can affix to the waist in several different ways --- some use clips to attach onto the belt or waistband, others have slots for your belt to secure the holster. Some are formed like a paddle that lies flat on the inside of the pants, and some use rare earth magnets to secure to an unbelted or weaker waistband. Generally speaking, on-the-waistband carry works well with many women's clothing styles, such as pants of all kinds, and skirts and shorts, but keep in mind that concealment outside the waistband requires larger, longer shirts or garments to effectively hide the gun.

When wearing a belt, which is preferred for better stability, I recommend you purchase a good sturdy leather belt, preferably one designed for holstering a gun, as they have inserts to provide a solid and steady 'platform' base for the holster to be secured. The belt must be wide enough to fully support and distribute the weight of the firearm

**Inside the waistband** carry, where the bulk of the firearm lies inside the waistband, is a very popular form of concealed carry for women. With this method, only the grip or butt of the gun needs to be covered and the firearm is very accessible and easy to draw. Most regular women's shirts will cover sufficiently and most pants can stretch to make the adjustment necessary to fit the firearm.

The *In The Waistband* holster by **The Well Armed Woman** solves the problems women typically have with in-the-pants carrying. It is reversible for right or left handed women, and has a deep tuck-able and adjustable clip so you can customize exactly where it sits on your waistline. You can also adjust the cant to your desired angle. A nice feature is that the clip is recessed to minimize any bulge.

The *Ava,* another in-the-waistband holster is a thermoplastic hybrid made to be worn inside the waistband featuring two clips for a broader platform. Typically worn in the small of the back.

The *Sticky Holster* is made of a revolutionary material that 'sticks' to you and your clothing using the tension created in your waistband to hold the holstered gun secure.

Exactly where you carry on the waistband is a personal choice. Comfort and ease of access are the key factors. Most common locations are on the strong side, (the same side as your shooting hand) in the front abdominal area, or towards the back just off the hip with the handle angled properly for an easy draw. Appendix carry is with the gun placed in front, between your belly button and your hip.

Many holsters are what are called 'tuck-able' which means that the holster clip has a slot to tuck your shirt into, in between the clip and the firearm itself. This is practical for women when wearing pants, slacks, or a skirt with a strong waistband or shorts. There are options made in leather, plastic and nylon.

## Undergarment Concealed Carry

Women's *compression concealment shorts* are a way for women to carry and conceal a handgun when they're wearing a skirt, slacks, gym shorts, sweat pants, jeans, or dress pants without a belt. The concealed holster is made from surgical grade elastic and sewn into a pair of authentic compression shorts and holds your firearm securely. They feature two holsters offering ambidextrous concealment and you can also carry spare magazines, or other important items on the other side. Because they are 'compression' you get a little extra shaping too!

The sling style *Pistol Pouch* by **Thundewear** is extremely comfortable as it is made from cotton. It is worn under your garments but over your underwear. The low, below the belly position makes for very good conceal-ability. This is great for when you are wearing scrubs or sweat pants with a waistband that allows for easier access. However it would be difficult to access the gun quickly if you have a belt and a zipper to contend with.

Belly bands and under-wraps are versatile and very comfortable methods of concealment that many women use effectively. You can wear these in many situations, whether dressed for work or going to the gym. They are made of heavy duty elastic with a Velcro closure. Most have two firearm slots: one for an automatic pistol and one for a revolver. It can have a pocket, which conceals important papers, cash, credit cards, as well as a slot for a spare magazine. It works great with medium and small frame revolvers and semi-automatic pistols. They can be worn high under the breasts or low on the hips for added versatility. Simply rotate to the desired location. In my opinion, the belly band is a great option. Its versatility allows for multiple carry locations.

The *Pistol Wear Sport* is designed for an active and athletic lifestyle. With this holster, the gun is fully encased to prevent slippage and to keep the gun from falling out during physical activity. It is made from a very comfortable, water resistant material. Enclosed holsters require additional practice as the grip is not exposed for optimum accessibility.

An issue when using belly bands and under wraps is the possibility of aiming the muzzle of your firearm at your torso when placing it in the holster. This is known as 'covering yourself'. Placing the firearm in the holster prior to putting it on is a good practice. It can be difficult to adjust or re-holster your firearm once the band or wrap is in place without compromising your non-dominant hand or torso, so caution is required when re-holstering.

### Underarm and Shoulder Holsters

Another option is a compression tank top. These 'undershirts' have holster pockets on both sides with thumb breaks, and hold the firearm just under the armpit. They are snug fitting to provide stability. These are best with V-neck shirts as you can simply reach down the collar to grasp the grip.

The **Pistol Wear** *Underarm Holster* is another under the arm option with removable/adjustable straps for versatility. Made from very comfortable breathable material it can be a cooler option. Like the **Pistol Wear** *Sport*, this holster is designed to prevent slippage and requires additional practice as the grip is not exposed for optimum accessibility.

### Ankle and Thigh Holsters

When wearing pants, the ankle holster can be a good option and can be worn quite comfortably all day long. These wrap around the ankle with a holster on the side. Many come with an optional calf support and some padding for added comfort. Worn with looser hemmed pant legs it can keep your firearm very well concealed without bumps and lumps in your clothing.

There are some challenges with ankle carry. One is that it is impossible to draw your gun while you are moving or running. The draw from standing can also be awkward, and practice is necessary. Thrusting your leg out to the side or front as in a lunge can make drawing faster from the standing position. This holster may be a good choice, however, for work and office settings where you will be seated most of the time.

The thigh holster is a great option when wearing dresses or skirts. The waistband with garter keeps it from sliding down. You can adjust the height to accommodate your hemline and surprisingly, when worn correctly, they are invisible, even when sitting. It is very important that the thigh holster is made of materials that can reliably hold the gun securely and comfortably. Thin or lacy holsters lack the necessary support and thickness to insure that the trigger cannot be accidentally engaged when holstering or adjusting your holster.

## Bra Holsters

These holsters are designed to attach to your bra in the center between the two cups or on the outer edge of the cup, under the arm. They offer easy access when wearing an un-tucked blouse, shirt or sweater. The *Flashbang* clasps the holster to the center of your bra, with the barrel and handle tucked slightly under the bra underwire. The *Marilyn* clips on the outside of the cup and the smoothest draw is through the top of the shirt.

To be blunt - the more you've got- the larger the firearm you can conceal and the better you can conceal it. So for those of you who are more well endowed this can be a very comfortable and effective form of concealed carry.

One concern is that the firearm can cover (the muzzle pointing unsafely) the non-shooting arm as it is pulled from the holster and raised to shoot. Practice and awareness are necessary with this form of holster.

## Pocket Holsters

Carrying your firearm in your pants or jacket pocket is an option, but jacket or vest carry makes it easy to become separated from the firearm, which of course makes for a serious safety issue. Pocket carry is only practical with very small firearms or very large pockets. There are many pocket holster styles and materials. The most important thing is that it covers the trigger guard area completely to prevent against accidental discharges. The pants you wear must also have enough room in the pockets to comfortably pocket the firearm. If you wear looser pant styles, or cargo pants with multiple pockets this may be a comfortable option for you.

A pocket holster is also necessary when carrying your firearm in any other bag or purse. It must cover the trigger guard to prevent you from accidentally pulling the trigger while reaching in your bag or purse. A purse specifically designed for concealed carry is preferred. These are discussed at length in the next chapter.

### Fanny Pack Style Holsters

A fanny pack holster has the look of an ordinary fanny pack but carries a concealed handgun in a hidden compartment in the back of the pack. This fanny pack style concealment holster allows you to carry a pistol or other protection device like pepper spray. These can be helpful when warm weather dictates dressing in light clothes. A handgun can be drawn from the concealed carry position very quickly. You pull the front of the bag with one hand to open the firearm compartment and draw with the other hand.

Fanny pack carry is very comfortable and looks appropriate in outdoor situations and large spectator events. Unlike purse carry, a properly designed fanny pack provides the quickest access to the firearm if you need it in a hurry, and as it is secured to your body so you are less likely lose it or have it snatched.

Fanny pack carry is a very good option for women because it is on your body. These can be worn with any clothing style. The key factor is that you need to keep it on your body at all times.

I have done a series of videos on many of the holsters to show you what they are like and exactly how they are worn. You may find them helpful. You can find these on the **The Well Armed Woman** website at **Thewellarmedwoman.com**.

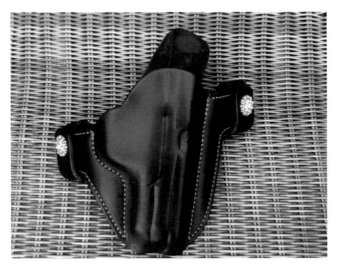

An example of a custom on the waist holster designed to attach to the belt with loops adorned with rhinestones. These "Build Your Own" holsters are available in multiple leather colors with dozens of threat color options for a large number of gun models. Orderable RH or LH

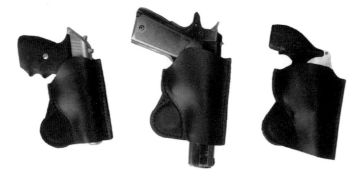

The Magnetic Holster is IDEAL for lighter weight pants and sweatpants or skirts with no belt. It uses a very powerful rare earth, neodymium magnet to secure to the waistband. Orderable in canted or cross-draw style as well as RH or LH draw.

The ambidextrous in-the-waistband holster is made from Kydex which is molded for specific gun models. The Well Armed Woman IWB holster features a recessed adjustable clip to lower the holster in your waistline.

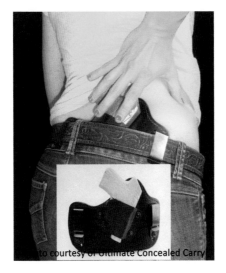

The Ava leather and thermoplastic hybrid holster is made to be worn inside the waistband. It features a soft leather back piece that conforms to the wearer's shape. The clips are adjustable and can be raised or lowered to create a total of 9 different cant/depth combinations. It is available in both RH & LH models

Photo courtesy of Undertech

These ambidextrous compression concealment shorts feature two identical holsters, one on each side so you can also carry spare magazines or documents on the other side. The full and snug fit also offer the added shaping benefit. Also available in nude.

*The Well Armed Woman Pistol Pouch* by Thunderwear is an all cotton 'pouch' that sits on the natural slope of the lower stomach/pelvic area. It comes in multiple holster sizes for a variety of gun sizes. It is extremely comfortable and best with stretch or loose waistbands.

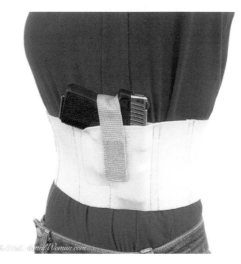

*The Well Armed Woman 4" Belly Band* is worn under clothing in a high, mid or low position and rotated to any position and is a great versatile holster option. It includes a removable thumb break strap.

*The Sport* is worn under your exercise or causal wear. This deep concealment holster fully encloses the gun to keep it from slipping or falling out during physical activity. It's breathable belt allows heat to pass through and is perspiration resistant. Offered in 2 holster sizes and extensions are available.

Photo courtesy of Undertech

The ambidextrous *Compression Concealment Tank*, conforms to any body type comfortably and does not restrict movement. It is extremely comfortable and holds the gun securely. It is also available in black and nude.

*The Underarm Holster by Pistol Wear* is a soft, breathable, perspiration resistant material. Removable and adjustable strap allows for all types of shirt collars. This holster fully encases the gun for almost print-less carry.

*The Well Armed Woman Ankle Holster* has been designed for a women's shorter calf and narrower ankle. It is available in 3 holster sizes and a variety of ankle sizes. It is available in both RH & LH models.

*The Well Armed Woman Thigh Holster*, above with removable waistband/garter worn exposed for display purposes, allows for both height adjustment and inside or outside the thigh wear. Available in two holster sizes and multiple thigh/waist sizes. It is available in both RH & LH mode

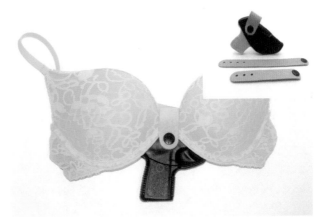

*The Flashbang* is a Kydex holster which snaps to the center of the bra. It can be worn high (shown) or low. It is available in many gun models and with three strap lengths to accommodate most bras. It is available in both RH & LH models.

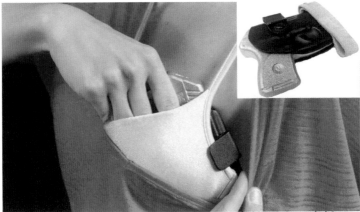

Photo courtesy of Ultimate Concealed Carry

*The Marilyn* bra holster is a Kydex holster that clips to the outer edge of the bra cup and the strap secures to the bra side strap for easy down the shirt collar draw. It is available in both RH & LH models.

Pocket holsters come in many different shapes, sizes, designs, and materials. The **Fun Print** holster comes in 5 fabrics and black nylon. Most importantly, a pocket holster must fully cover the trigger and trigger guard.

**The Concealed Carry Pack** adds a little more style to the traditional fanny pack. There is plenty of room for your handgun, 2 magazines and even your phone. Wear with your belt or use the belt strap included. Adjust belt strap and wear cross body too. Available in black and 2 patterns.

# 6 THE CONCEALED CARRY PURSE

The concealed carry purse: people either love them or they hate them. The decision to carry your firearm in a concealed carry purse is yours to make and there is no right or wrong answer, although many fiercely counsel against this popular mode of carry. This is likely for two reasons --- one, there is serious risk anytime our guns are not on our bodies, and two, it limits our ability to respond as quickly as possible when every second could count. Awareness and practice is key with this form of carrying.

Do I carry in a concealed carry purse? Yes, sometimes I do. Why? Because there are times when, if I didn't, I wouldn't have my gun with me, and that is not an option for me (as long as it is legal.) I know myself - I know my capabilities - and I practice!

With the proper purse, meticulous awareness, and lots of practice drawing and shooting, a concealed carry purse can be a valid option for you.

**Making The Decision To Use A Concealed Carry Purse**

When choosing to carry in a concealed carry purse, here are some questions you might ask yourself in making this decision:

1. Am I forgetful?
2. Have I left my purse behind in the last 6 months, in the restroom, a restaurant or store?
3. Am I around small children regularly who might have access to my purse?
4. Am I willing to carry my purse cross-body to minimize risk of someone snatching it?
5. Can I keep it on me and store it properly when it must be off my body?
6. Will I vow to always have my gun in a holster in a designated compartment of the purse?
7. Am I disciplined enough to practice the special techniques for drawing from a concealed carry purse? (You may very likely need to shoot through the purse to avoid losing precious seconds)

If you can't answer these questions with confidence, this method of concealed carry is probably not right for you.

**What To Look For In A Concealed Carry Purse**

Remember, your concealed carry purse is an important piece of equipment and it plays a key role in your effective concealed carry system. The quality and construction must not be sacrificed when making your selection. It must have a dedicated compartment for the gun. One that will carry nothing else but the holstered gun. Items such as keys, pens or lipstick tubes could enter the trigger guard and result in a negligent discharge. The holster should secure to the inside of the compartment wall and allow for the gun to be positioned for your easy access.

Many purses have straps that are reinforced with a steel cable to prevent someone from 'slashing' the straps to steal your purse.

A quality concealed carry purse will be made with a material thick enough that the gun will not print, which means the outline of the gun will not be visible through the material.

The zippers must also be of the best quality. The gun compartment zipper should slide open smoothly and easily, while pulling downwards.

I am seeing more and more concealed carry purse options coming on the market. Although stylish, many are missing some of these important features.

### Practice With Your Concealed Carry Purse

Learning to draw or fire your gun from your concealed carry purse can only be mastered through diligent practice. As with any holster, your ability to remove the gun safely and get into a strong firing position is critical. In an emergency situation you may lose precious time locating, freeing, and drawing your gun from a purse. Spend some time with your UNLOADED GUN moving and drawing it, following the rules of gun safety and those of dry fire practice. When we are under great stress, we are not thinking about our training tips; we default to what we have practiced and what has become habit. The more systematic your motions in training the better your body will be at naturally following those same motions in an emergency.

Consistency is key to safely carrying your firearm in a purse. Carry your concealed carry purse the same way at all times, with the zippers and/or compartment in the same location, and practice this way. Train yourself to always pick it up and position it in the same place on your shoulder. You will want to attach the holster (typically with Velcro) in the same position in the compartment all the time. You want it in the right position and angle for you to easily grasp the grip once you open the compartment.

Likewise, unzip or open the holster compartment the same way every time. Turn the purse to safely point the gun in the right direction - the muzzle of the gun should never point at any part of your body. Turn slightly and point the muzzle corner of the purse away from you and in a safe direction. Grasp the grip of the gun with your strong hand, keeping your trigger finger straight along the side of the gun and not in the trigger guard, and pull firmly to remove it from the holster while simultaneously pulling the purse away from the gun with your weak hand. This will clear the gun and allow you to get into firing position.

You may also want to practice having to shoot through the purse. In this scenario, the gun needs to be removed enough from the holster to get a good firing grip on the gun and to free the trigger guard so you can fire if necessary. Because you are not aiming the gun as you normally would, learning how to point and shoot is recommended. Point and shoot is the act of simply raising the gun in the direction of your target and using your instinctive pointing ability to aim. Time is not taken to sight the target with the sights on your gun. This of course takes practice.

Depending on where you do your live-fire practice and what the policies are at the range, (many ranges unfortunately do not allow drawing from a holster or purse in this instance) it is ideal if you can practice with your purse during live-fire practice. If possible, you can even buy a cheap purse that is similar in style to your concealed carry purse and actually practice shooting through the bag. IMPORTANT: make sure the bag is empty and that there is nothing that could cause a ricochet or splinter and do harm to anyone or anything. This is why it is SO IMPORTANT to use a concealed carry purse that has a specific compartment that is specifically designed to hold the gun and nothing else. If you use an ordinary purse, loose objects can either get caught in the trigger guard area, hinder your aim, or cause you or others injury.

# 7 CONCEALED CARRY IN THE SUMMER

The hot weather of summer can make concealed carry quite a challenge, and for many women, this results in leaving the gun at home. Unfortunately, criminals don't take the summer off, so we must find ways to carry in every season.

I wish I had the one true simple fix for you, but I don't. Here, however, are some suggestions that can help you better and more comfortably conceal as the temperatures increase and your clothing decreases! Remember though, there are times, as an armed woman, you will have to make some adjustments and sacrifices to accomplish carrying effectively and safely throughout the year.

## Go Looser and Longer

Thankfully, light, loose clothing never goes out of style. Looser, lighter clothing is not only more comfortable, it's cooler because it allows the air to circulate. Wear a long cotton shirt with your summer shorts and skirts to easily conceal your firearm in the waist or on the belt. Patterned shirts and dresses work well to camouflage and minimize the appearance of any bulges. In-the-waistband carry is a great option. The *Magnetic* is a very popular holster for the simple reason that it requires no belt or heavy waistband to secure itself to. If wearing summer dresses, the bra holsters (mentioned above) are a good bet, as is the *Pistol Wear Under Arm*, which is made with breathable fabric.

## Go Deeper

Summer weight pants, shorts and skirts mean lighter and weaker waistbands, which can make on-the-waist or in-the-pants carry more difficult. Try a holster that isn't dependent on the waistband such as the *Pistol Pouch* that 'buries' the firearm down on the pelvic area. Your belly band worn low and on your hips can also be a solution. Keep in mind however that going deeper brings with it some challenges --- mainly accessing your gun quickly and safely. Practice these draws regularly with your unloaded gun.

## Go Smaller

Although not the ideal solution, as we don't want to give up firepower if we don't have to, carrying a smaller gun in the summer months is an option and is better than not carrying any gun at all. If you can afford a second gun, the very small and compact semi-automatics and lightweight revolvers are very easy to hide. Some are now so slim that they don't create a bulge, (and who needs more of those?) You may want to research the available holsters for these models prior to purchasing to make sure the type of holster you want to wear is available for it. Keep in mind that smaller, lighter guns will have quite a bit more recoil to contend with. They simply don't have the weight and size necessary to absorb the energy.

# 8 CONCEALED CARRY FOR LARGER WOMEN

Concealed carry for larger women brings up some additional issues that only exacerbate the already challenging problem of finding holsters that can be worn comfortably, discreetly, safely and allow for effective access to the gun should the need arise. A large bust makes reaching for a firearm difficult and sometimes impossible if crossing the body is necessary. A fuller middle (including pregnant bellies!) also interferes with reach and accessibility. Clothing styles and options that accommodate concealed carry are limited, which only adds to the problems and frustrations. For some women, the combination of these challenges makes typical methods of concealed carry so uncomfortable and frustrating that they give up trying.

Each woman naturally will have her own set of challenges because every woman's body is unique. But the concealed carry issues faced by larger women are significant and the topic is often neglected. Here, I will attempt to summarize the problems and solutions shared by hundreds of women who frequent **The Well Armed Woman** site. Again - there is no single solution to the various problems larger women have with concealed carry, but you can take comfort in the fact that, as a larger women, you are not alone and that many women share your frustrations. Hopefully you will find a suggestion or two here that will help you carry your firearm safely and comfortably. All women need to push through and overcome their particular obstacles, because if your gun is not on or with you - it can't protect you.

## The Most Common Issues of Concealed Carry For Larger Women

### Larger Bust

For buxom women the primary issue is reach. They simply can't get around their breasts to get to their gun, whether it's in a shoulder, cross-body, an on-the-waistband holster; even a bra holster poses difficulties. One might assume that a bra holster would work well, given that large breasts create sufficient 'hiding space' for a gun, but a majority of larger women report that bra holsters don't work for them, explaining that the gun 'gets lost' and is extremely hard to draw.

### Wide Around The Middle

Being wide around the middle restricts the ability to reach the holstered concealed carry gun, especially with bra holsters and on or in-the-waistband holsters (whether appendix or cross body). The need to wear looser stretch pants with elastic waistbands also limits the possible options for on or in-the-waistband holsters as they need the support of either a sturdy wide belt or a substantial and tight waistband. Having a large middle also makes it tough to access an ankle holster. Another common frustration of concealed carry for larger women is that the grip of the gun digs into them in most on-the-waist forms of carry.

## Short Waist

Many women have a shorter waist than men do. This makes drawing from an on-the-hip holster difficult, as there is not enough room to fully clear the firearm without running a fist into the underarm or breast. And the more of you there is in that shorter distance, the tougher this becomes. The distance is simply not sufficient for an effective draw. Most on-the-hip holsters ride too high, which only makes things worse. When you factor in elastic or weak waistbands and it becomes almost impossible.

## Some Suggestions For Concealed Carry For Larger Women from Larger Women

So, what can you do to make concealed carry more comfortable and effective for you as a larger woman? This depends on your climate, and what your particular physical issues are. But there are a couple of common areas of agreement among the women we polled. The majority found the belly band to be a very good option, siting its ability to be rotated to any position around the middle. Belly bands can also be worn high or low on the middle, so the user can find the location most comfortable for her and which provides the easiest access to her gun.

An alternative suggested by very large chested women was using an inside-the-waistband holster but clipping it to the top of the bra near the armpit, the top corner of the breast, not under it. In this case a simple reach through the collar of the shirt allows for easy access.

Carrying the firearm on the waist with a loose fitting cover shirt, or in the pants, off the back of the hip, more toward the small of the back, was another successful position for many of the larger chested, wider middle women. In this case the middle and the bust do not come into play, which allows for smoother access. Whenever holstering on the back, however, a woman must be hyper alert to her surroundings as she may be more vulnerable to another person gaining access to it from behind.

A rubberized pocket holster, which will stick firmly to clothing without the need of a clip, was another popular option for in-the-waistband carry. Many women reported to me that because of the non-slip qualities of the rubber you can place the firearm in any location and it stays put, making it ideal for stretch waistbands.

Another suggested option is a magnetic outside-the-waistband holster, which instead of a metal clip uses a very strong magnet that locks shut over the waistband. No belt is required because the strength of the magnet provides the necessary support. Also available are paddle holsters, which slide down the inside of the pants, acting as a brace to keep the holster in place when no belt is available.

For larger women who happen to have a long waist, a very positive solution is to wear low-rise pants. The lowered waistband will increase the distance between the grip of the gun and the armpit. Adjusting the location to just off the hip (front or back) and adjusting the cant to a steeper angle for easier access is also effective.

For women whose middles were 'in the middle', the most successful reported option was in-the-waistband appendix-style carry. Because the gun is carried in the fleshy front (in front of the hip bone) this was found to be a very comfortable carry position, providing good access to the waist area.

Many women who deal with a large bust and shorter waist issues suggested the ankle holster, but this option is reported as ineffective for women who are larger in the middle as noted earlier, because it can be difficult to access.

A final option for larger women would be carrying in a concealed carry purse or fanny pack. As discussed in Chapter 6, carrying a concealed gun in an external bag takes an extra dose of awareness and responsibility, but for many women it can be the difference between carrying and not carrying.

Our ability to carry a concealed gun is a powerful equalizer for women in an assault situation. For many large women, running away or running for cover may not be a realistic option. She must be able to access her gun quickly, safely and with the skill necessary to defend herself. That requires at least three things: the gun must be with her, it must be holstered in a manner and location that SHE can manage, and she must be well-trained and prepared to draw and use it effectively. Hopefully some of the above suggestions will help larger women to conceal carry successfully and confidently.

# 9 USING THE RESTROOM WHILE CARRYING

Going to the ladies room...taking a potty break...powdering your nose...whatever you call it - we ALL have to do it! The problem is, what in the world do you do with your concealed firearm when you have to 'go'?

There is quite a bit of confusion and not a lot of discussion on this 'interesting' topic. So, what should you do? You don't want anyone in the next stall to see your firearm, freak out and call 911 when you're simply answering Mother Nature's call. You don't want it to fall on the floor and slide over to into the next stall, and you certainly don't want to do anything that could risk an accidental discharge. So what *do* you do?

The answer is quite simple. The less you do the better! Anytime your remove your firearm from its holster you create risk. A well made in-the-pants or on-the-waist holster should hold your firearm snug, even if you accidentally turn it upside down. If yours doesn't - get a new one. Not everyone likes a thumb break but here is an instance where they come in handy. Keep your hand on the HOLSTERED firearm as you carefully slide down your pants. Keep the top of your pants up off the floor and out of view of 'neighbors'. If you're wearing a belt, this is even more important as once you undo your belt - the weight of whole package takes on a mind of its own.

Problems arise when you remove the firearm to get comfortable. Some of you are placing it on the toilet paper dispenser, the back of the toilet and even hanging it by the trigger guard on the hook on the door. These are not safe solutions and yes, even the most responsible and conscientious gun owners can leave and forget their firearms behind.

Bra and belly band holsters are the most 'potty friendly'. With these holsters this challenge is eliminated. For those of you who carry in your purse, as awkward as it may be, place your purse on your lap, or even hang it over your body cross body style.

If for some reason not addressed here you MUST remove the firearm from your body, keep it holstered and hold it or keep it on your lap while you're 'busy'.

All of this effort may seem cumbersome, uncomfortable and even a pain in the neck. But it's all part of responsible and safe gun ownership. If you really think about it, we are very lucky to even have the right and opportunity to be a little uncomfortable this way. So... give thanks and go take care of business!

# 10 THE IMPORTANCE OF PRACTICE WITH YOUR HOLSTERS AND YOUR GUN

Being a woman, you probably carry your gun in a variety of holsters in a variety of locations. It is essential that you can comfortably, safely and quickly draw your gun from each of your holsters. Regular practice should be built into your daily routine. Perhaps practice a few draws (UNLOADED) as you dress and prepare your holster each day.

The more different locations you carry in, the harder it may be to recall exactly where your gun is the moment you need it. It is recommended that you very consciously tell yourself out loud where you are carrying your gun and remind yourself throughout the day. "Today I am carrying my gun in my bra holster". "I am eating my lunch with my gun in my bra holster". This might seem silly, but, unlike men, who carry their guns in the same location in the same holster every day, you may be using multiple holsters worn in multiple locations, and in situations where every second counts, you need to be able to draw in an instant, without thinking. Practice drawing and shooting your gun is a cornerstone of safe gun ownership. If your range allows, spend some time practicing drawing and shooting from a variety of distances and positions. Practice is your key to success. Owning the best gun and carrying it in the best holster means nothing if you can't get your gun out and on target quickly and safely.

## Training To Improve Your Shooting Skills

Spending some quality time practicing with your gun is one of the most important things you can do, not only when you first purchase your gun, but on an ongoing basis. Becoming thoroughly familiar with your gun - its feel, its weight and how it works - is a major step toward becoming a Well Armed Woman and gaining the confidence that comes with knowing that you can protect yourself, your home, and your loved ones.

We don't like to think about it, but there may come a day when you will need to use your gun in self-defense. When and if that moment comes, you won't have the luxury of a warning. You will need to rely on your instincts, and you will need to make decisions under extreme stress. This won't be the time to get acquainted with your gun! You do not want to be fumbling with it and trying to remember how to use it when your life is at stake.

It is natural, especially if this is your first gun, to feel rather awkward in the beginning, but trust me, this passes quickly with practice. The very first place to start with any new gun is the owner's manual. Read it from cover to cover and become familiar with the details of your specific piece of equipment. If for any reason you did not receive one, get online and find it on the manufacturer's website or call the gun store or the manufacturer directly to get one.

Before practicing with or handling ANY gun, you and only you are responsible to check and verify that it is not loaded and that it is empty of any ammunition. In the case of a semi-automatic pistol, verify that the magazine is removed. EVEN if someone you know and trust tells you or shows you that it is empty - check it YOURSELF! Visually confirm it by looking down the barrel from the rear end and check the chambers or magazine well, and then physically verify by placing your finger into the barrel and chambers of a revolver or the magazine well of a semi-automatic. Even when you have verified that your firearm is empty, part of your training MUST be to always handle your gun, whether empty or loaded, following The Four Rules of basic self-defense safety:

1. All guns are always loaded.
2. Never let the muzzle cover anything you are not willing to destroy.
3. Keep your finger off the trigger until your sights are on the target.
4. Be sure of your target and what is beyond it.

As with any other skill, the key to success with a firearm is practice, practice, practice! You will want to constantly practice to improve your skills and become a better shot. Your ability to hit your target may just save your life. There are three forms of practice that should be part of your ongoing relationship with your gun.

1. **Instruction** - If you start this new endeavor learning to handle and shoot a gun correctly, you are less likely to form bad habits that are tough to break later and that just may cost you your life in an emergency. Nothing can replace training with a qualified professional. They are trained to assist you, the new shooter, to learn how to safely and effectively handle your gun. I encourage you to find and attend a good basic shooting class staffed with qualified firearms instructors. If you are a more experienced shooter, learning more advanced skills and fine tuning those you already have is also recommended. There are many classes available on a variety of gun skills. The truth is, all gun owners are ALWAYS TRAINING. You can search for qualified female firearms instructors on **The Well Armed Woman** website

2. **Dry-Fire Practice** - Dry-fire is a generic term for practicing at home with an UNLOADED gun. It does not necessarily mean only pulling the trigger. It can refer to practicing reloads, drawing,

sighting or most any other skill you need to master with your gun. You may think that not much can be accomplished by practicing with an empty gun, but the fact is, improvement will be significant. Dry-fire is an essential component of learning to shoot well. All top shooters incorporate a significant amount of dry-fire into their training. But use caution, many negligent shootings are caused by people, even experienced shooters, dry-firing in a careless manner and mixing live ammunition with dummy rounds.

Before you get started *each and every dry-fire practice time:* READ AND FOLLOW THE BELOW RULES

**Prepare**:

Remove to the best of your ability anything that would cause you to be distracted. Turn of the TV or IPod, turn off your cell phone and/or the ringer of the home phone, lock your front door, remove or turn off anything that potentially could cause you to be distracted in any way. If there are others in the home, let them know you are not to be interrupted (except for an emergency of course). If for any reason at anytime during your practice you are interrupted, you must re-start these dry-fire practice safety steps.

**Unload**:

Unload your firearm and then unload it again! Visually check the cylinder or chamber twice. Use your fingers to manually check the firearm at least two times to ensure that all rounds have been removed. In the case of a revolver, pull the cylinder fully outward and slowly spin the cylinder to check all chambers.

**Move:**

Remove all ammunition from the room. That is correct - take all of the removed rounds and any other ammunition and put it in another room. Select a container, a specific one that you will use each and every time, to place the removed ammunition in. Count each round as you place them in this container to verify that each round removed from the cylinder or magazine is accounted for.

**Select:**

Select or prepare your backstop, taking into consideration those who are in the home and those who live nearby. Your interior wall and most exterior walls will not stop a bullet if you for any reason have an negligent discharge. An appropriate backstop may be a concrete wall (keep in mind the risk of ricochet), a full bookshelf, or other item that could stop or absorb a fired round. There are some products that are specifically designed for dry-fire practice, such as portable ballistic material 'pads' that will absorb an accidental misfire and can be placed anywhere or hung on the wall. If you cannot set up a safe backstop in your home, do not dry-fire.

**Begin:**

Decide the amount of time and the specific skills you will practice ahead of time. 10 - 15 minutes is recommended. A training check-list can be very helpful, and there are a number of online dry-fire tools to track your practice sessions. Just before you begin your skill practice, tell yourself out loud "I am starting dry-fire practice". This verbal cue is an important discipline.

**Finish:**

Complete your practice by telling yourself out loud "Dry-Fire practice is over." This verbal and audible proclamation will help keep you disciplined and help to prevent you from 'trying one more'. When you are done, you are done. Remove any dummy rounds and verify that your firearm is unloaded. Take down your target and put your dry-fire gear in its proper place. Take a short break between your dry-fire practice and the reloading of your firearm with live ammunition. A pause between these two actions is necessary, as you have just focused on pulling the trigger and doing so with the confidence that there was no live ammunition in the firearm. You, of course, do not want to get these two actions confused. So this pause is necessary to be safe.

Practice dry-firing your gun at home at least once a week.

3. **Live-Fire Practice** - Nothing can build skill and confidence like shooting your gun with a real target, real ammunition, real recoil and real noise. Practice live rounds at the range at least once a month with your defensive handgun, for a minimum of 50 rounds each time. Shooting practice is not just about shooting at a single target in a single place, over and over again. Depending on where you are shooting, indoors or out, there are an endless variety of drills and fun targets to make your experience challenging and exhilarating. Find a women's shooter group such as a **Well Armed Woman Shooting Chapter,** who meet monthly to learn and train together. There isn't anything more fun than training with friends.

While the above types of practice are the most important, there are also some wonderful instructional books and videos that can be a useful complement and follow-up to your practice regime. They certainly can't replace personalized formal instruction, but you can greatly enhance your training with them.

Research supports the fact that women are excellent students. Women not only seek instruction, they pay attention better, follow directions better, and apply learned principles and techniques better. As women, we juggle everything and everybody. We put the needs of others before our own needs. In reality, our personal safety and protection should be a priority. Why? Because if you are not here – you are letting down the people who count on you. Make time, schedule time, and commit to taking the time to practice with your gun.

Let's keep in mind that, in addition to the awesome responsibility that it entails, shooting is also fun. In fact it becomes more fun the more you shoot and the better you get. Personally, I love the power. I love the bang! But I love getting better best of all.

*The Well Armed Woman*

## 11 FINAL THOUGHTS

You are on your way to becoming a truly Well Armed Woman. You are doing your homework and making the necessary commitments to carry a firearm responsibly. As such, you represent women gun owners all across the country. This is quite a responsibility and makes you an ambassador for us all.

You took on this great responsibility the day you purchased your first firearm. By taking the sacred right of gun ownership seriously, by knowing and following the laws, diligently practicing with your gun and adhering to the rules of safety, you are setting an example for other women to follow. You are also in a unique position to influence what others think about guns and gun ownership. Those around you will form opinions and make voting decisions based on what they learn from you.

So let's go forth, you and I, as ambassadors for smart, safe, and savvy women gun owners everywhere. Let's do our best to be good examples of how we can protect ourselves and our loved ones, and keep our rights as citizens safe at the same time. I'm proud to join forces with you!

13779988R00033

Made in the USA
San Bernardino, CA
06 August 2014